X-RATED DRINKS

More than 250 of the Hottest Drinks Ever Made

Ray Foley

SOURCEBOOKS, INC.
NAPERVILLE, ILLINOIS

Published by Sourcebooks, Inc.
P.O. Box 4410, Naperville, Illinois 60567-4410
(630) 961-3900
FAX: (630) 961-2168
www.sourcebooks.com

Originally published in 1998

Library of Congress Cataloging-in-Publication Data
Foley, Ray.
  X-rated drinks : sizzling cocktails for steamy nights / Ray Foley.
    p. cm.
  Previous ed.: The Hymie Lipshitz X-rated drink book. 1998.
  Includes bibliographical references and index.
  ISBN-13: 978-1-4022-0772-3 (alk. paper)
  ISBN-10: 1-4022-0772-7 (alk. paper)
  1. Cocktails. I. Lipshitz, Hymie. Hymie Lipshitz X-rated drink book. II.
Title.

TX951.F597 2006
641.8'74–dc22
                                                          2006020837
             Printed and bound in the United States of America.
                          DR 10 9 8 7 6 5 4 3

Dedication

This book is dedicated to all bartenders, those X-tra special people, and my X-tra loving partner and that X-tra Special Person, Ryan Peter Foley.

"Let's have wine and women, mirth and laughter, sermons and soda-water the day after."
—Byron

"Let's have a great time, a lot of fun, and laughter, drink to laugh and have fun, but drink in moderation."
—Lipshitz

Preface

The proverbial "everybody and his brother," and maybe his mother too, has a favorite drink recipe. That's something I've learned over more than twenty years behind the bar as a "pouring professional."

A lot of people and their brothers (but not usually their mothers too, not unless the family is on the order of the Borgias of Renaissance history) also seem to know what I call "X-rated" drink recipes, with racy names. That really shouldn't surprise anyone, since from the time of the pyramid-building Pharaohs on down, spirits have been used as a liquid facilitator of, ah, amatory purposes. People have always been horny—in other words, people have always done in real life what liquor ads in the last few years picture them doing, getting set for seduction, and they have turned to alcoholic beverages as an aid, as mind and spirit softeners.

The Romans, for example, swore by wine from grapes grown near the Tyrrhenian Sea mixed with spices from the farthest outposts of the empire. And just like today's situation with regard to the perfect martini, everybody, and I do mean everybody, had his or her favorite recipe for said concoction. It was a golden age for both orgies and aphrodisiacs.

So now you're probably asking, do aphrodisiacs work (as to whether orgies do, I leave to your own doubtless impeccable breeding and discretion)? Well, allow me to ask you, did oysters work the last time you served them for specifically erotic ends? Or Häagen-Dazs rum raisin ice cream? I mean, hey, if coating yourselves in butterscotch sauce and then rolling around in sprinkles helps, don't look funny at me!

This is why it doesn't really matter, despite the pretty far-fetched claims I've heard made for a lot of these recipes, if X-rated drinks work as sexual aids or not. You can have fun even if nothing much happens. You will at the very least enjoy a tasty treat, an unfamiliar combination of flavors that you may well wind up adopting as your mixed drink of choice. And if you request one of these drinks at the right affair, say in lieu of your pastor's favorite Sherry at the annual church social, you may also enjoy everyone else's shock and consternation.

There's something grade-schoolish in us all that gives us a kick out of just pronouncing the names of these drinks. It's the same kind of glee we felt when we dumped a toad down a girl's book bag in sixth grade or said our first foul curse word.

That's fine, as long as that's as far as it goes. I like to drink, but I know better than to drink to excess. Liquor may indeed be an aphrodisiac, but let us also face up to the fact that it is, in large enough amounts, a dangerous depressant.

Other than that, I'd like to stress just how much fun this book has been to assemble. I've heard and borrowed from bartenders and premise patrons from literally all over America, each one making more grandiose promises for the sexual efficacy of their particular favorite than the last one. Were they all kidding? Were any? And does it matter if the drink recipes they supplied hold up anyway?

Personally, I doubt it, so my sincere thanks go out to all those who helped make this book what it is, some of whom are thanked elsewhere in the dedication and others in sum total the proverbial "those too numerous to mention." Well hell, you all know who you are, and some of you told me in no uncertain terms that even under the most favorable circumstances you didn't want your names mentioned. Gang, I'm as good as my word here.

For now, however, it's back to work. And, I don't drink while I'm working, no matter where, when, or how. Instead, go have one on me and think kindly of me when drinking it. I won't mind. Rather, I'll be flattered. And, in the case of this book, imbibing is very much the sincerest form of flattery.

Again, thank you and enjoy yourselves. And, like Dr. Ruth Westheimer does, I wish you all "good sex," particularly if lubricated by this volume's premium potables.

Your friend,

Ray Foley

ABSOLUT SEX

1/2 oz. Absolut Kurant
1/2 oz. melon liqueur
1/2 oz. cranberry juice
1/2 oz. lemon-lime soda

Pour over cubed ice.

ABSOLUT ULTIMATE SHOOTER OR (ABSOLUT APHRODISIAC)

A raw oyster or clam in a shot glass with a shot of Absolut Peppar, topped with a spoonful of cocktail sauce or a dash of horseradish and a squeeze of lemon.

Shoot it down!

ADIOS MOTHER

1/2 oz. vodka
1/2 oz. blue curacao
1/2 oz. gin
1/2 oz. rum
2 oz. sweet & sour mix

Build. Top with club soda.

After
Hot Sex

AFTER HOT SEX

1 1/2 oz. Bartenders Hot Sex
3 oz. coffee

Serve in a cup with a cigarette.

———— • ◆ • ————

ANGEL PISS

1 1/2 oz. scotch
2 oz. Perrier
lime, squeezed

Shake and strain. Shake slowly or, better, stir.

———— • ◆ • ————

ANGEL'S BLUSH

1/4 maraschino liqueur
1/4 Benedictine
1/4 heavy cream
1/4 crème yvette

Pour into a very thin glass in order, so that the ingredients don't mix. Depending on the social occasion "1/4" can mean anything from an ounce to a quart.

Angel's Tit

ANGEL'S TIT

1 1/2 oz. dark crème de cacao
3/4 oz. cream

Pour the crème de cacao into a large cordial glass. Take a spoon and invert it over the top of the liquid. Pour cream slowly over the back of the spoon and the cream will float on top. Put a pick through a cherry and lay it on top.

———————— ● ◆ ● ————————

ANTI-FREEZE

1 oz. blue curacao
1/2 oz. spearmint schnapps
dash lemon-lime soda

Shake and strain.

APHRODITE'S LOVE POTION

4–6 ice cubes
1 1/2 oz. Metaxa brandy
1–2 dashes Angostura bitters
4–6 oz. pineapple juice
1 maraschino cherry
1 thin orange slice

Combine all ingredients and stir. Garnish with a cherry and an orange slice. This hasn't failed yet.

———— •◆• ————

APPLE BLOW

1 1/2 oz. applejack
1 tbs. lemon juice
1 egg white
1 tsp. superfine sugar
1 oz. apple juice
6 ice cubes
6 oz. club soda, chilled

Combine all ingredients in a shaker. Strain and pour over ice.

APPLE KNOCKER

1 1/2 oz. vodka
2 tbs. cider
1 tsp. lemon juice
1 tsp. strawberry liqueur
3–4 ice cubes

*Combine all ingredients in a shaker and strain
into a glass. Don't drink this in New York.*

———— •◆• ————

ARISE MY LOVE

1 oz. green crème de menthe
champagne, chilled

Layer crème de menthe and champagne in a flute.

A.S.S.

1/3 oz. Absolut vodka
1/3 oz. spearmint schnapps
1/3 oz. sambuca

Serve in a shot glass.

—— • ◆ • ——

BALL BANGER

1 1/2 oz. ouzo
fill orange juice

Build in a highball glass over ice cubes. Bang away.

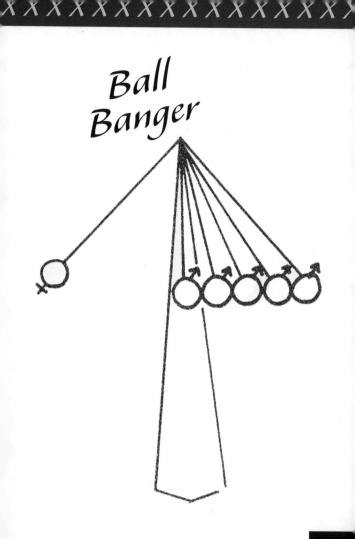

BALL OR HEAD COCKTAIL

1/2 oz. gin
1/2 oz. French vermouth
1/2 oz. Italian vermouth
dash Pernod

Shake with cracked ice and strain into a chilled cocktail glass. Twist a lemon peel over the glass and serve with a stuffed olive. Take your choice!

BASTARDO

1 oz. dry vermouth
1 oz. sweet vermouth
1/2 oz. brandy
2 dashes bitters
club soda
1 slice lemon

Pour dry vermouth, sweet vermouth, brandy, and bitters over rocks in an old-fashioned glass. Add soda and garnish with a lemon slice.

BEAUTY AND THE BEACH

1 oz. light rum
1 oz. Southern Comfort
1 tbs. Grand Marnier
1 tsp. lemon juice
1–2 dashes orange bitters
3–4 ice cubes

Combine in a shaker and strain into a glass. No sand please.

———— • ◆ • ————

BEND-ME-OVER EASY

1 oz. amaretto
3/4 oz. pineapple juice
1/4 oz. sweet & sour mix

Shake with ice and strain.

BEND-ME-OVER I

1 1/4 oz. Absolut vodka
3/4 oz. Disaronno amaretto
1 1/2 oz. sweet & sour mix

Chill. Serve straight up or on the rocks.

David's Restaurant & Lounge
Chattanooga, TN

———— •◆• ————

BEND-ME-OVER II

1 1/2 oz. amaretto
1 1/2 oz. vodka
1 1/2 oz. sweet & sour mix
1 1/2 oz. orange juice

Serve in a highball glass over ice.

BETTER THAN SEX I

1/2 oz. Frangelico
1/2 oz. Irish cream liqueur
1/4 oz. Grand Marnier
1/2 oz. Kahlúa

Fill with cream (10 oz. glass). Shake and serve on the rocks. Maybe, maybe not!

———— •◆• ————

BETTER THAN SEX II

1/2 oz. cognac
1/2 oz. Frangelico
1/2 oz. Irish cream liqueur
1/4 oz. Grand Marnier
1/4 oz. coffee liqueur
4 oz. cream

Shake with cubed ice.

BETTER THAN SEX III

1 oz. vodka
1/2 oz. raspberry liqueur
1/2 oz. sweet & sour mix

Shake with ice and strain.

• ◆ •

BETWEEN THE SHEETS I

1 oz. light rum
1 oz. brandy
1/2 oz. Cointreau
dash lemon juice
3–4 ice cubes

Combine all ingredients in a shaker and shake vigorously. Strain drink into a glass. An all-time great place to be when drinking this one.

Better than Sex

Between the Sheets

BETWEEN THE SHEETS II

1/2 oz. cognac
1/2 oz. dark crème de cacao
1/2 oz. cream
dash Angostura bitters
1 tsp. sugar

Shake well and strain into a cocktail glass. Use a lemon peel for garnish.

BITCH

1 1/2 oz. cinnamon schnapps
orange juice

Serve on the rocks. One of these is enough.

BITCH ON WHEELS I

1 1/2 oz. Gordon's gin
1/2 oz. Martini & Rossi dry vermouth
1 tsp. DeKuyper white crème de menthe
3-4 ice cubes

Combine all ingredients in a shaker and shake vigorously. Strain into a glass. Don't drink and drive.

— • ◆ • —

BITCH ON WHEELS II

1/4 oz. Martini & Rossi extra dry vermouth
1 oz. Bombay gin
1/4 oz. Pernod
1/4 oz. white crème de menthe

Shake and strain.

Bitch on Wheels

B.J. SHOOTER

1/2 shot Baileys Irish cream
1/2 shot Grand Marnier

Top with a dot of whipped cream.

— • ◆ • —

BLACK DEVIL

4 parts Bacardi light rum
1 part dry vermouth
1 black olive

*Combine rum and vermouth in a mixer glass with
cracked ice, stir, and strain into a cocktail glass.
Add a black olive.*

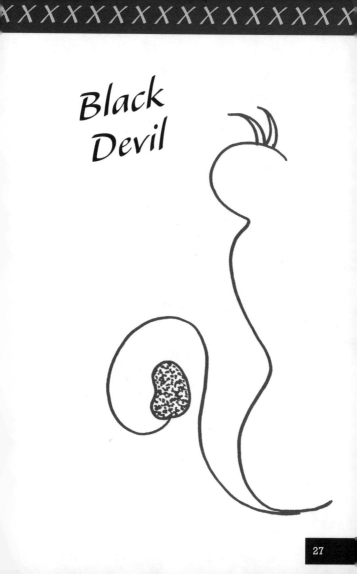

Black Devil

BLEEDING HEART

1/2 Aalborg Akvavit
1/2 cherry brandy

Pour ingredients in the order listed above. Serve in a rocks glass.

———— •◆• ————

BLONDE BOMBSHELL

1 oz. vodka
1 oz. brandy
3 dashes DeKuyper Apple Barrel schnapps
3 dashes DeKuyper Harvest Pear schnapps

Shake well.

BLOODY AWFUL

1/2 oz. Chartreuse
1 1/2 oz. Metaxa brandy
3 oz. tomato juice

Shake and throw away.

———— •◆• ————

BLOODY MARIA

1 1/2 oz. white tequila
3 oz. tomato juice
1/2 oz. lemon juice
dash Worcestershire sauce
2–3 drops Tabasco sauce
salt and pepper to taste
ice

Shake all ingredients with ice and strain into a glass. Olé!

BLOODY MARY

1 1/2 oz. vodka
3 oz. tomato juice
dash lemon juice
1/2 tsp. Worcestershire sauce
2–3 drops Tabasco sauce
pepper and salt

Shake with ice and strain into an old-fashioned glass over ice cubes. A wedge of lime may be added.

BLOW JOB I

3/4 oz. Kahlúa
3/4 oz. Chambord

Shake and strain into a pony glass. Top the rim of the glass with whipped cream. Place your hands behind your back to drink. Lift the glass only with your mouth.

BLOW JOB II

1/2 oz. Kahlúa
1/2 oz. Baileys Irish cream
1/2 oz. Stolichnaya

Layer in the above order. Top with whipped cream.

———— •◆• ————

BLOW JOB III

Equal parts:
  Kahlúa
  Baileys Irish cream
  whipped cream

Build. Place your hands behind your back. (Use of hands would make it a "hand job.") Use your mouth to pick up the shot glass and swallow.

BLUE DEVIL

1 1/4 oz. gin
1/2 oz. blue curacao
1/2 oz. sweet & sour mix

Blend with crushed ice. Pour into a cocktail glass. Garnish with a lemon twist.

— • ◆ • —

BOLERO

1 1/2 oz. Rhum Barbancourt
1/2 oz. Calvados
2 tsp. sweet vermouth
dash bitters

Stir. Serve straight up or with ice.

BOSOM'S CARESS

1 oz. brandy
1/2 oz. triple sec or curacao
1 egg yolk
1 tsp. grenadine
3-4 ice cubes

Combine all ingredients in a shaker. Strain into a glass. Serve in a large cup or cups.

— • ◆ • —

B.S. ON THE ROCKS

1 oz. Bacardi light
1 oz. peach or pear schnapps

Serve over ice in 4–5 oz. rocks glass.

BRAIN HEMORRHAGE

3 parts Irish cream
1 part peach schnapps
dash grenadine

Combine in a shot glass.

———— •◆• ————

BUN WARMER

3/4 oz. apricot brandy
3/4 oz. Southern Comfort
hot cider

Add the brandy and Southern Comfort in a coffee mug. Fill the mug with hot cider. Garnish with a cinnamon stick.

Bun Warmer

CALIFORNIA HOT SEX

1 oz. Bartenders Hot Sex
1/2 oz. California brandy

CHOCOLATE ORGASM

1/3 oz. dark crème de cacao
1/3 oz. amaretto
1/3 oz. Irish cream

Serve in a shot glass.

CLIMAX COCKTAIL

1 1/2 oz. applejack
1/2 oz. French vermouth
1/2 tsp. grenadine
1/2 tsp. lemon juice

Shake with crushed ice, strain into large cocktail glass, and grate nutmeg on top. Relax and have a smoke.

———— •◆• ————

CLIMAX

1 shot Southern Comfort
2/3 shot Kahlúa
splash half-and-half

Shake.

COCO AMOR

1 oz. CocoRibe
1/2 oz. amaretto
1/2 oz. lemon juice

Shake well with ice and strain into a chilled cocktail glass with a sugar-frosted rim. Love is in the glass.

COLD KISS

1 1/2 oz. blended whiskey
1/2 oz. peppermint schnapps
2 tsp. white crème de cacao
3 oz. crushed ice

Combine all ingredients in a shaker and strain into a glass. This might warm you up!

COLORADO M F

1 oz. tequila
1 oz. Kahlúa

Put in a collins glass filled with ice. Add milk, shake, and add a splash of cola.

COME IN HOT TUB

3/4 oz. Kahlúa
3/4 oz. Baileys Irish cream

Kahlúa first. Fill a soda straw with Baileys and let go so it will come to the top through the Kahlúa.

Come in
Hot Tub

COMFORTABLE FUZZY SCREW

1 1/2 oz. vodka
1/2 oz. Southern Comfort
1/2 oz. peach schnapps
4 oz. orange juice

Serve over ice.

———— •◆• ————

COMFORTABLE FUZZY SCREW UP AGAINST THE WALL

1 1/2 oz. vodka
1/2 oz. Southern Comfort
1/2 oz. peach schnapps
4 oz. orange juice
splash Galliano

COMFORTABLE SCREW

1 oz. vodka
3/4 oz. Southern Comfort
4 oz. orange juice

Serve over ice in a highball glass.

— •◆• —

CORKSCREW

1 oz. light rum
1/4 oz. dry vermouth
1/4 oz. peach liqueur
1 slice lime

Shake ingredients with ice, strain into a chilled cocktail glass, and garnish with a lime slice.

Corkscrew

Cuban
Screw

CORPSE REVIVER

1 oz. cognac
1/2 oz. Calvados or DeKuyper Apple Barrel
  schnapps
1/2 oz. Italian vermouth

*Stir with cracked ice, strain into a cocktail glass,
and garnish with a twist of lemon.*

———— •◆• ————

CUBAN SCREW

1 1/2 oz. rum
orange juice

*In a highball glass filled with ice, add rum, and
fill with orange juice. A favorite in Miami.*

CUTTHROAT

1 1/4 oz. Finlandia cranberry vodka
orange juice

*Add vodka to a tall glass with ice. Fill with
orange juice.*

— • ◆ • —

DECEIVER

1 oz. tequila
1/2 oz. Galliano

*Build in a rocks glass with cubed ice. This one will
fool you.*

DEEP THROAT

1 1/2 oz. vodka
1/4 oz. Tia Maria or Kahlúa

Top with whipped cream.

———— •◆• ————

DEVIL COCKTAIL

3/4 oz. brandy
3/4 oz. French vermouth
3 dashes curacao
2 drops bitters

Stir with cracked ice and strain into a cocktail glass. Garnish with a cherry.

Devil
Cocktail

DEVIL'S DELIGHT

1/2 oz. brandy
1/2 oz. vodka
1/4 oz. Grand Marnier
1/4 oz. curacao
juice of 1 lime or 3 oz. sweet & sour mix

Shake well.

DEVIL'S TAIL

1/2 oz. golden rum
1 oz. vodka
1/2 oz. lime juice
1/4 oz. grenadine
1/4 oz. apricot liqueur
lime peel

Add ingredients in a mixer glass filled with ice and shake. Pour into a chilled, deep champagne glass. Twist a lime peel and drop into the glass.

DIRTY MOTHER I

1 oz. Kahlúa
1 oz. Sauza tequila
milk or cream to fill

Strain over ice into a rocks or highball glass.

————— •◆• —————

DIRTY MOTHER II

1 1/4 oz. brandy
1/2 oz. Kahlúa
1 oz. Sauza tequila

Build in a rocks glass with crushed ice.

DIRTY VIRGIN

1 1/2 oz. Tanqueray gin
1/2 oz. dark crème de cacao

Shake, serve over rocks, and clean up your act.

— ◆ —

DISAPPOINTED LADY

3/4 oz. brandy
3/4 oz. Tia Maria
3/4 oz. orange juice
3/4 oz. crème de noyeaux
grenadine

Shake and strain into a glass. Add a dash of grenadine and sprinkle nutmeg on top. This will cheer her up.

Disappointed Lady

DO BE CAREFUL COCKTAIL

1/2 oz. gin
1/2 oz. Cointreau
1/2 tsp. grenadine
1/2 tsp. lemon juice

Shake with crushed ice and strain into a chilled cocktail glass.

DRY HOLE

1 oz. light rum
1/2 oz. apricot brandy
1/2 oz. Cointreau
1/2 oz. lemon juice
3 ice cubes
8 oz. club soda, chilled

Combine all ingredients except soda in a shaker. Fill glass with crushed ice and strain into a glass. Top with soda. This will get you wet in the right spot.

ERECTION

1 part 151 Don Q
1 part mango juice
1 part strawberry juice
1 part orange juice
1 part Captain Morgan spiced rum (on top)

Ramon E. Urbina
Aguas Buena, PR

— • ◆ • —

FALLEN ANGEL COCKTAIL

dash Angostura bitters
2 dashes crème de menthe
juice of 1 lemon or 1/2 lime
2 oz. dry gin

Shake well and strain into a glass.

FIRST LOVE

2/3 champagne
1/3 gin
1 tsp. sugar
2 dashes Cherry Heering

Shake and serve with ice very gently.

FIRST NIGHTER

1/2 oz. gin
1 tsp. Dubonnet Blond
1 tsp. maraschino liqueur or Kirsch
3–4 ice cubes
2–3 oz. dry sparkling wine, chilled
1 strip orange peel

Combine in a mixing glass and stir well. Slowly pour down the throat of your new love.

FLAME OF LOVE

1/2 oz. Tio Pepe dry Sherry
1 1/2 oz. vodka
1 four-inch strip orange peel
3 oz. crushed ice

Pour Sherry into a glass to coat the inside of the glass. Place ice cubes in the glass and add vodka. Add a twist of orange peel. This one will light you up.

FOLEY'S FIZZ

1/2 oz. Spanish fly
1/2 oz. prune juice

You come or go. (Note: "Spanish Fly," actually a powdered beetle, is not available in the U.S.A., but is widely found throughout Latin America.) It's a joke!

FOREPLAY

1 oz. VAT 69
1/2 oz. triple sec
1 oz. sweet & sour mix
1/4 oz. Onzaza syrup

California Charlie's favorite!

——— •◆• ———

FORNICATION

1/2 oz. Irish cream liqueur
1/2 oz. Tia Maria

Mix together slowly and then shake like hell.

FREDDY FUDDPUCKER

1 1/4 oz. tequila
2 1/2 oz. orange juice
1/2 oz. Galliano

Build in a Collins glass with ice and float Galliano.

FRENCH FOAM

1/2 oz. brandy
1/2 oz. Kirschwasser
1 1/2 oz. sugar syrup
3-4 dashes Angostura bitters
6-8 oz. dry sparkling wine, chilled
1 scoop lemon or orange sherbet

Combine all ingredients. Float a scoop of sherbet on top. This one keeps you coming safely.

French
Foam

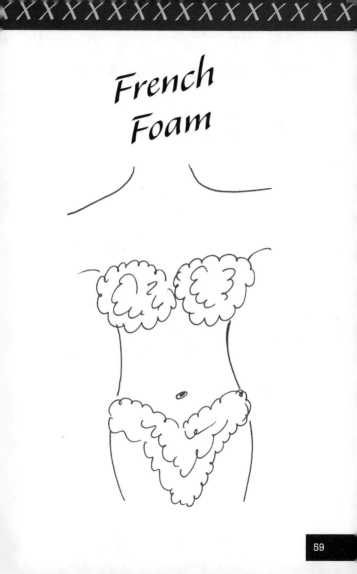

FRENCH HOOKER SHOOTER

1/2 shot vodka
1/2 shot Chambord
splash sweet & sour mix

Stir and strain.

———— •◆• ————

F.U.

1 1/2 oz. Frangelico
2 1/4 oz. club soda

Serve in a tall glass. Stir with your middle finger.

F "UN" HOT

1 1/2 oz. Absolut Peppar vodka
1 1/2 oz. DeKuyper cinnamon schnapps

Serve in a metal cup. Drink very, very, very slowly.

———— •◆• ————

FUZZY BALLS

1/2 oz. peach schnapps
1/2 oz. vodka
1/2 oz. Midori
1 1/2 oz. grapefruit juice
1 1/2 oz. cranberry juice

You'll be itching for another.

FUZZY NAVEL

1 1/2 oz. DeKuyper Original Peachtree
  schnapps
orange juice

*In a glass with ice, add schnapps and fill with
orange juice.*

—————— •◆• ——————

GIN & BEAR IT

1 oz. Gilbeys gin
1/2 oz. beer

Serve in a shot glass. Grin and drink it fast.

GIN AND SIN

1/2 oz. orange juice
1/2 oz. lemon juice
1 oz. gin
1–2 dashes grenadine
3–4 ice cubes

Combine all ingredients in a shaker and strain into a glass.

———— •◆• ————

GONE TOMORROW

2 oz. gin
2 drops lemon juice

In an old-fashioned glass with crushed ice, add gin and lemon juice. Garnish with just the stem of the cherry!

GORGEOUS

1 oz. Grand Marnier
1 oz. amaretto

Serve in a rocks glass with cubed ice.

——— • ◆ • ———

GORILLA FART SHOOTER

1/2 shot Bacardi 151
1/2 shot Wild Turkey 101

Stir and strain.

GORILLA SWEAT

2 oz. white or gold tequila
1 tsp. butter
1 whole clove
6 oz. boiling water
1 cinnamon stick

Combine all ingredients except cinnamon stick in a hot mug. Pour and stir with a cinnamon stick. This is a hairy one!

———— •◆• ————

GREEK SCREW

1 1/4 oz. ouzo
1/2 oz. orange juice

Serve over rocks.

GREEK WAY

1 1/2 oz. ouzo
1/2 oz. Metaxa brandy

Serve in a shot glass.

———— •◆• ————

GREEN DEVIL

1 1/2 oz. gin
1/2 oz. lime juice
1/4 oz. green crème de menthe
2 sprigs mint

*Shake gin, lime juice, and crème de menthe well
with ice. Strain over ice in a chilled old-fashioned
glass. Garnish with sprigs of mint.*

GREEN PUSSY

1 oz. white rum
Equal parts:
  sweet & sour mix
  melon liqueur

Serve in a rocks glass over ice.

———— •◆• ————

GREEN WEENIE

1/2 oz. peppermint schnapps
1/2 oz. Midori

Layer.

G-SPOT

1/8 oz. vodka
1/4 oz. Licor 43
1/2 oz. Chambord
dash sweet & sour mix
dash soda

Shake and strain.

HAIR RAISER

1/3 anisette
1/3 brandy
1/3 triple sec

Shake well. Serve in a shot glass.

HANKY PANKY COCKTAIL

2 dashes Fernet Branca
1/2 oz. Italian vermouth
1/2 oz. dry gin

Shake well and strain into a glass. Squeeze an orange peel on top.

HAPPY HOOKER

1/3 oz. Tia Maria
1/3 oz. Drambuie
1/3 oz. Grand Marnier

Layer in a shot glass. Shoot it and hold in your mouth as long as you can.

HARD DICK

3/4 oz. Absolut vodka
1/2 oz. Frangelico
splash soda

*Put the recipe into a shaker can filled half way
with ice. Shake and strain into a 2 oz. cordial
glass.*

—— • ◆ • ——

HARI-KARI

1/2 brandy
1/2 Cointreau
juice of 1/2 an orange

Shake well.

HARVEY BOWEL BANGER

1 oz. vodka
1 oz. prune juice

It gets you high and hits you low!

———— •◆• ————

HEAD BANGER

1 oz. straight bourbon
1 oz. Southern Comfort

Stir with cubed ice and strain.

HEAT WAVE

1 oz. Myers's rum
1/2 oz. triple sec
1/2 oz. Rock & Rye
1 drop lemon juice

Mix in a toddy glass; fill with boiling water. Garnish with a slice of orange, a whole clove, and a stick of cinnamon.

———— • ◆ • ————

HERE TODAY

2 oz. gin
2 drops lemon juice

Put gin in an old-fashioned glass with crushed ice, add lemon juice, and garnish with a cherry intact on a stem.

HI-RISE

1 oz. vodka
1/4 oz. Cointreau
2 oz. orange juice
1 oz. sweet & sour mix
1/4 oz. grenadine

Blend with crushed ice. Pour into a bucket glass.

HOLE-IN-ONE COCKTAIL

1 1/2 oz. Scotch whisky
3/4 oz. vermouth
1/4 tsp. lemon juice
dash orange bitters

Shake well with cracked ice. Strain into a rocks glass.

HONEY DO ME

1 1/2 oz. Barenjager honey liqueur
1/2 oz. melon liqueur

Shake with cubed ice. Serve with or without ice.

———— •◆• ————

HOP-SKIP-AND-GO-NAKED

1 oz. Absolut vodka
1 oz. Tanqueray gin
juice of 1/2 lime
beer to fill

Serve over ice. Bare it all for all.

HORNY BULL

1 1/2 oz. tequila
3 oz. orange juice
1 oz. prepared lemonade
1/2 oz. grenadine

Combine all ingredients in a blender with ice and blend until firm. Garnish with an orange wedge and a cherry. Don't let these catch up with you.

———— •◆• ————

HOT BUTTERED COMFORT

1 1/2 oz. Southern Comfort
1 lemon slice
4 oz. hot water
1 cinnamon stick
1 tsp. butter

Combine all ingredients except butter in a warm mug. Float butter on top and stir with a cinnamon stick. Perfect with the Greek way.

HOT PANTS I

1 oz. peach schnapps
1/4 oz. Absolut Peppar vodka

Combine over ice.

———— • ◆ • ————

HOT PANTS II

1 1/2 oz. tequila
1/2 oz. peppermint schnapps
1 tbs. grapefruit juice

Shake.

HOT PUSSY

1/2 oz. cinnamon schnapps
2 drops Tabasco
1 oz. orange curacao

Shake over ice. Serve straight up.

———— •◆• ————

HOT SEX

2 oz. Bartenders Hot Sex

Serve on the rocks.

HOT SEX PATTY

1 oz. Bartenders Hot Sex
1 oz. peppermint schnapps

Shake with ice. Serve straight up or on the rocks.

———— •◆• ————

HOT SHOT

1 cube beef bouillon
boiling water
1 1/2 oz. tequila
seasoning, as desired

Dissolve the cube of beef bouillon in a mug of boiling water. Add the tequila and season to taste.

IN THE SACK

2 oz. cream Sherry
2 oz. apricot nectar
3 oz. orange juice
1/2 oz. lemon juice
1/2 slice orange

Shake ingredients well with ice, strain into a 14 oz. glass, and garnish with an orange slice.

———— •◆• ————

INTERNATIONAL STINGER

1 oz. Metaxa brandy
1/2 oz. Galliano

Build in a rocks glass with cubed ice.

IRISH HOT SEX

1 oz. Irish Whiskey
1 oz. Bartenders Hot Sex

Serve straight up or on the rocks.

— • ◆ • —

ITALIAN HOT SEX

1 oz. sambuca
1 oz. Bartenders Hot Sex

Serve straight up or on the rocks.

ITALIAN STALLION

3/4 oz. Galliano
3/4 oz. crème de banana
1 1/2 oz. heavy cream

Blend with crushed ice. Pour into a wine glass.

———— •◆• ————

JACK MEOFF

1 1/2 oz. applejack
1/2 oz. Midori
3 oz. lemon-lime soda

Shake first two ingredients gently. Add lemon-lime soda. Serve straight up.

JACK-OFF

1/2 oz. Jack Daniel's whiskey
1/2 oz. Baileys Irish cream

Put the recipe into a shaker filled 1/3 with ice. Shake and strain into a 1 1/4 oz. shot glass.

———— •◆• ————

KISS N' TELL

1 oz. Calvados or apple brandy
1 oz. sloe gin
1 tsp. lemon juice
1 egg white
3–4 ice cubes

Combine all ingredients in a shaker. Strain into a glass.

KISS OFF

1 oz. Gilbey's gin
1 oz. Cherry Marnier
1 tsp. Martini & Rossi dry vermouth
3-4 ice cubes

Combine all ingredients in a shaker and shake vigorously. Strain into a glass.

———— •◆• ————

KISS

1 1/4 oz. vodka
3/4 oz. chocolate cherry liqueur
1/4 oz. heavy cream
1/2 fresh strawberry

Combine all ingredients in a shaker. Strain into a glass. Top with a strawberry. Bring this to your lips.

KISS-ME-QUICK-HIGHBALL

1 1/2 oz. Pernod
4 dashes curacao
2 dashes bitters
club soda

Put Pernod, curacao, and bitters into a highball glass filled with ice. Top with club soda.

———— •◆• ————

LA PUSSY

1/3 Bacardi rum
1/3 Cointreau
3 dashes DeKuyper Apple Barrel schnapps
1/3 brandy

Shake well.

LADIES COCKTAIL

1 1/2 oz. Calvert extra whiskey
2 dashes absinthe
3 dashes anisette
dash bitters

Stir well with ice. Strain into a glass. Serve with a piece of pineapple on top.

———— •◆• ————

LADY GODIVA

2 oz. brandy
1 tsp. sugar
2 dashes triple sec
juice of 1/4 lemon
juice of 1/2 lime

Shake well.

Lady
Killer

LADY KILLER

1 1/4 oz. gin
3/4 oz. sweet vermouth
3/4 oz. dry vermouth
3 dashes orange bitters

Combine ingredients in a mixer with ice. Stir well, strain into a glass, and serve.

———— •◆• ————

LIMP DICK

1/2 oz. Southern Comfort
1/2 oz. amaretto
1/2 oz. white crème de menthe
1/4 oz. Courvoisier

Shake and strain.

LITTLE BASTARD

1 oz. Bacardi rum
1 oz. orange juice
1/2 oz. pineapple juice

Shake well. Fill with lemon-lime soda.

· ◆ ·

LITTLE DEVIL

3/4 oz. gin
3/4 oz. gold rum
1 tsp. triple sec
juice of 1/2 lemon

Combine ingredients with ice, shake, and strain into a glass with ice.

LITTLE DEVIL COCKTAIL

1 oz. lemon juice
1 oz. Cointreau
1/4 oz. Bacardi rum
1/3 oz. dry gin

Shake well and strain into a glass with crushed ice.

—— • ◆ • ——

LOLITA

3 oz. burgundy wine
2 oz. sweet & sour mix

Shake and serve in a tulip glass (8 oz.) filled with ice. Garnish with a lemon slice and cherry.

LOVE BIRDS

1 1/2 oz. vodka
2 oz. sweetened lemon juice
dash dark rum
1/2 oz. grenadine

Mix in a blender with 1 cup cracked ice and pour into an old-fashioned glass. Add a cherry.

———— • ◆ • ————

LOVE POTION

3/4 oz. Remy Martin
1/4 oz. Disaronno amaretto
1/4 oz. Frangelico
2 oz. cream
dash Rose's grenadine

Shake and strain over crushed ice in a cocktail glass.

LOVER'S COCKTAIL

2 oz. sloe gin
1 egg white
1/2 tsp. lemon juice
1/2 tsp. raspberry juice

*Shake with ice and strain into a cocktail glass.
Can also fry in a pan.*

————— •◆• —————

LOVER'S NOCTURNE

1 1/2 oz. Absolut vodka
1/2 oz. Drambuie
dash bitters

*Shake all ingredients well with crushed ice and
strain into a cocktail glass.*

Lover's Cocktail

LOVING CUP

2 oz. brandy
1 pint claret (red wine)
1 oz. triple sec
6 oz. carbonated water
1 tsp. powdered sugar

Fill a large pitcher with ice and stir in the ingredients. Fill the one you love with this!

————— • ◆ • —————

MAIDEN'S BLUSH

1 1/2 oz. dry gin
1 tsp. triple sec
1 tsp. grenadine
1/4 tsp. lemon juice

Shake with ice and strain into a cocktail glass. Garnish with a lemon slice.

Maiden's
Blush

MAIDEN'S BLUSH
COCKTAIL I

dash lemon juice
4 dashes orange curacao
4 dashes grenadine
2 oz. dry gin

Shake well and strain into a glass.

MAIDEN'S BLUSH
COCKTAIL II

1/3 oz. Pernod
2/3 oz. dry gin
1 tsp. grenadine

Shake well and strain into a glass.

MAIDEN'S PRAYER
COCKTAIL I

1 1/2 oz. Tanqueray dry gin
1/2 oz. triple sec
1 oz. lemon juice

*Shake with ice and strain into a cocktail glass.
Garnish with a lemon slice.*

MAIDEN'S PRAYER
COCKTAIL II

1 1/2 oz. orange juice
1 1/2 oz. lemon juice
1/2 oz. Cointreau
1/2 oz. Beefeater dry gin

Shake well and strain into a glass.

Maneater

MAIDEN'S PRAYER
COCKTAIL III

1/2 oz. Lillet
1/2 oz. Gordon's dry gin
1/2 oz. Calvados or apple brandy

Shake well and strain into a shot glass.

—— •◆• ——

MANEATER

1 1/2 oz. Southern Comfort
2 dashes orange bitters
1 1/2 oz. brandy
3-4 ice cubes
3 oz. crushed ice

*Combine all ingredients except crushed ice in a
shaker. Place crushed ice in a glass and pour.
Don't sip this one.*

MEISTER-BATION

1 oz. Jagermeister
1/2 oz. crème de banana
1/2 oz. cream
2 1/2 oz. piña colada mix

Shake with cubed ice and strain.

MENAGE-A-TROIS

1 oz. Alize
1 oz. Alize Red Passion
1/2 oz. Stoli Ohranj vodka
1 1/2 oz. orange juice
1 1/2 oz. cranberry juice

Pour Alize, Red Passion, and Stoli Ohranj. Add cranberry and orange juice. Garnish with an orange slice. Serve chilled in a martini glass.

Menage-A-Trois

MEXICAN SCREW

1 1/2 oz. tequila
orange juice

*In a highball glass filled with ice, add tequila and
fill with orange juice. Go south of the border.*

MIND ERASER

1 part vodka
1 part Kahlúa
1 part club soda

*Shake all but club soda and strain into a shot
glass.*

MOFO

1/2 oz. cranberry juice
1/2 oz. vodka
1/2 oz. peach schnapps
3 oz. milk

Serve over ice. Do not stir.

MONKEY GLAND

1 1/2 oz. gin
1 tbs. fresh orange juice
few drops Benedictine
few drops grenadine

Stir with ice in a mixing glass. Strain into an old-fashioned glass over plenty of ice.

MUFF DIVER

1 1/4 oz. crème de cacao
1 1/4 oz. cream
juice of 1 lime
juice of 1 lemon

Shake well.

MUFF RIDER

2 oz. Sake
1 oz. light rum
3 oz. pineapple juice
bitter lemon soda

Shake Sake, rum, and pineapple juice with ice.
Strain into a 14 oz. glass filled half way with ice.
Fill the glass with bitter lemon soda.

MULTIPLE ORGASM

1/3 shot coffee liqueur
1/3 shot Irish cream
1/3 shot amaretto
splash half-and-half

Top with tequila.

—— • ◆ • ——

MUSTANGE RANCH
FREEBEE

3/4 oz. Bacardi silver rum
1/2 oz. sweet & sour mix
1/4 oz. grenadine
1 oz. grapefruit juice

Quick shot in a blender with crushed ice. Pour in
a champagne glass.

MY PLACE OR NO PLACE

3/4 oz. Gilbey's gin
1/2 oz. crème de cassis
1/2 oz. Rose's lime juice

Mix in a blender with crushed ice. Serve in a champagne tulip glass. Garnish with a lime wheel and float a small, red straw.

—— •◆• ——

NAKED LADY

1/4 part Bacardi rum
1/2 part Martini & Rossi sweet vermouth
4 dashes DeKuyper apricot brandy
2 dashes grenadine
4 dashes lemon juice

Shake well and strain into a cocktail glass. Wow! Set this one up.

My Place or No Place

Nude El
Cocktail

NAKED MARTINI

2 oz. gin or vodka

No vermouth at all. Can be served straight up or on the rocks.

———— •◆• ————

NUDE EL COCKTAIL

1/2 oz. dry Bombay gin
1/2 oz. cognac
1/2 oz. Dubonnet
1/2 oz. Chartreuse

Shake with cracked ice and strain into a chilled cocktail glass.

ONE EXCITING NIGHT COCKTAIL

1 oz. orange juice
1/3 oz. French vermouth
1/3 oz. Italian vermouth
1 1/3 oz. Plymouth gin

Shake well and strain into a port wine glass. Squeeze a lemon peel on top. Frost the edges of the glass with sugar.

—————— •◆• ——————

OPENING NIGHT

1 1/2 oz. American blended whiskey
1/2 oz. Martini & Rossi dry vermouth
1/2 oz. strawberry liqueur
3–4 ice cubes

Combine all ingredients in a mixing glass and stir well. Strain into a glass.

ORGASM I

1 oz. Disaronno amaretto
1 oz. Baileys Irish cream
3-4 ice cubes

Combine all ingredients in a shaker and strain into a glass.

ORGASM II

3/4 oz. Absolut vodka
3/4 oz. Kahlúa
3/4 oz. Baileys Irish cream

Blend ingredients with ice. Strain after blending and pour into a prechilled cocktail or stemmed glass. No garnish.

ORGASM III

1/2 oz. Kahlúa
1/2 oz. Baileys Irish cream
1/4 oz. Disaronno amaretto

Layer in the above order.

———— • ◆ • ————

ORGASM IV

1 part Disaronno amaretto
1 part Kahlúa
1 part Baileys Irish cream
1 part cream

Shake and strain into a shot glass.

PARTY GIRL

1 1/2 oz. dry vermouth
1 tbs. gin
1/2 oz. crème de cassis
2-3 oz. crushed ice

*Combine all ingredients and pour into a glass.
Everyone should try this one.*

———— •◆• ————

PASSION PUSSY

2 oz. heavy cream
1/8 oz. grenadine
1 1/2 oz. Grand Marnier

Shake. Serve on the rocks.

Peep
Show

PECKERHEAD

1 oz. amaretto
1 oz. Yukon Jack
3 oz. pineapple juice

Put the recipe into a shaker filled half way with ice. Shake and strain.

— • ◆ • —

PEEP SHOW

1 oz. Dubonnet
1 oz. brandy
1/2 oz. Pernod
juice of 1/2 lime

Shake well.

PENIS COLAROUS

1/4 oz. Coco Lopez cream of coconut
1/4 oz. Leroux banana liqueur
1/2 oz. CocoRibe
1/4 oz. peach schnapps
3 oz. pineapple juice

Blend. Mix. Stir. Shake. Swallow.

———— •◆• ————

PERFECT SCREW

1 1/4 oz. pear schnapps
3 oz. orange juice
1/4 oz. vodka

Pour over rocks and shake, and shake, and shake, and shake.

PHILLIPS SCREWDRIVER

1 1/2 oz. vodka
1/2 oz. milk of magnesia
2 1/2 oz. orange juice

Serve over rocks. Stay near a toilet if you dare drink it.

———— •◆• ————

PINK PANTIES

1/2 oz. gin
1/4 oz. triple sec
1/4 oz. grenadine

Chill and strain into a shot glass.

Pink
Pussy

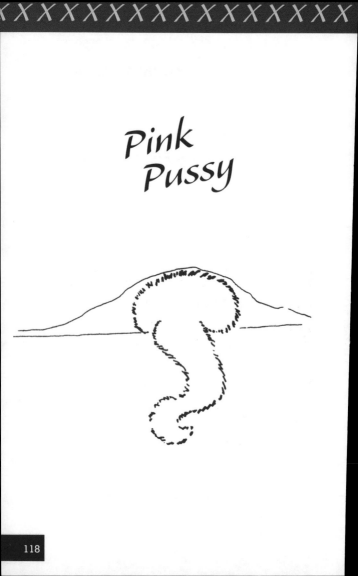

PINK PUSSY

1 oz. Campari
1/2 oz. peach brandy
4-6 oz. bitter lemon soda
6-8 ice cubes

Combine all ingredients and stir well. Tastes so sweet!

———— •◆• ————

PINK PUSSYCAT

1 1/2 oz. gin
3/4 oz. grenadine
1 egg white
3-4 ice cubes

Combine all ingredients in a shaker and strain into a glass.

PINK TWAT

2 oz. vodka
1/2 oz. Rose's lime juice
splash sweet & sour mix
splash grenadine

Put the recipe into a shaker filled half way with ice. Shake and strain.

———— •◆• ————

POND SCUM

1 oz. vodka
3 oz. club soda
1/2 oz. Baileys Irish cream

Float Irish cream on top and watch David Letterman.

PURPLE HOOTER I

1/2 oz. vodka
1/2 oz. black raspberry liqueur
1/2 oz. cranberry juice
splash club soda

Shake and strain vodka, black raspberry liqueur, and cranberry juice. Top with a splash of club soda.

—— • ◆ • ——

PURPLE HOOTER II

1 1/2 oz. lemon vodka
1/4 oz. Chambord
1/2 oz. triple sec

Stir with cubed ice and strain.

PURPLE HOOTER III

2/3 oz. vodka
1/3 oz. Chambord
1/3 oz. sweet & sour mix

Stir with cubed ice and strain into a shot glass.

———— •◆• ————

PURPLE KISS

1 1/4 oz. gin
3/4 oz. lemon juice
3/4 oz. crème de noyeaux
dash cherry brandy

Shake and strain into a cocktail glass.

PURPLE MASK

1 oz. vodka
1 oz. grape juice
1/2 oz. white crème de cacao

Shake with ice and strain into a cocktail glass.

PURPLE PASSION

1 small cluster of grapes
3 ice cubes
1 1/2 oz. Smirnoff vodka
3 oz. grapefruit juice
3 oz. grape juice, chilled

Place grapes in a glass. Add vodka and juices. Stir and serve.

PUSSYFOOT

1 oz. lemon juice
2 oz. orange juice
1 tsp. grenadine
1 cherry

Shake thoroughly with cracked ice and pour into a wine glass with ice. Decorate with a cherry.

———— • ◆ • ————

QUICKIE

1 oz. bourbon
1 oz. light rum
1/4 oz. triple sec

Shake with cracked ice and strain.

RATTLER

1 1/2 oz. gold or white tequila
2–3 oz. grapefruit juice
splash triple sec
juice of 1/4 lime
ice

Mix ingredients in a tall glass filled with ice. Add a wedge of lime.

———— •◆• ————

RED PANTIES

1 oz. vodka
1 oz. peach schnapps
1/2 oz. grenadine
2 oz. orange juice

Put the recipe into a shaker filled half way with ice. Shake and strain.

RED SILK PANTIES

1 oz. vodka
1/2 oz. peach schnapps
2 oz. cranberry juice

Layer.

―――――― • ◆ • ――――――

ROYAL SCREW

2 oz. cognac
2 oz. orange juice

Fill with champagne. Build over ice.

Red Silk Panties

RUM SCREW

1 shot Bacardi light rum

Fill with orange juice. Shake.

———— •◆• ————

RUSSIAN HOT SEX

1/2 oz. Stolichnaya vodka
2 oz. Bartenders Hot Sex

Shake with ice and serve.

S.H.I.T.

1/4 oz. sambuca
1/2 oz. Bartenders Hot Sex
1/2 oz. Irish Mist
1/4 oz. tequila

Shake above. Serve in a shot glass.

SALOME'S COCKTAIL

1/2 oz. French vermouth
1 1/2 oz. dry gin
1/2 oz. Dubonnet

Shake well and strain into a glass.

Salome's Cocktail

SCREAMING ORGASM I

1/2 oz. Baileys Irish cream
1/2 oz. vodka
1 oz. Kahlúa

Put the recipe into a shaker filled half way with ice. Shake and strain.

———— • ◆ • ————

SCREAMING ORGASM II

1/2 oz. vodka
1/2 oz. Baileys Irish cream
1/2 oz. Kahlúa
1/2 oz. cream

Shake and strain.

SCREAMING ORGASM III

3/4 oz. Absolut vodka
3/4 oz. Kahlúa
3/4 oz. Baileys Irish cream
3/4 oz. amaretto

Blend ingredients with ice and pour into a prechilled rocks glass.

———— •◆• ————

SCREW 'UM UP

2 oz. light rum

Build in highball glass over ice cubes. Fill with equal amounts of orange juice and lemon-lime soda.

SEX AT MY HOUSE

1/2 oz. Disaronno amaretto
1/2 oz. Chambord
1 oz. pineapple juice

Shake and strain.

— • ◆ • —

SEX IN THE DIRT

1/2 oz. Southern Comfort
1/2 oz. amaretto
1/2 oz. crème de cassis
2 oz. orange juice

Shake with cubed ice and strain.

Sex in the Parking Lot

SEX IN THE PARKING LOT

1/2 oz. vodka
1/2 oz. Chambord
1/2 oz. apple schnapps

Stir with cubed ice and strain.

SEX IN THE SNOW

1 oz. melon liqueur
1/2 oz. coconut rum
1/2 oz. 151 proof rum
2 oz. cream of coconut
3 oz. pineapple juice

Blend with ice until smooth.

SEX ON THE BAR

3/4 oz. Chambord
3/4 oz. Stolichnaya vodka
1/2 oz. Grand Marnier
2 oz. pineapple juice

Hank Millar
Boston, MA

SEX ON THE BEACH I

3/4 oz. Absolut vodka
3/4 oz. Midori
3/4 oz. Chambord
2 oz. pineapple juice

Serve chilled on the beach, by the pool, or anywhere.

Sex on the
Beach

SEX ON THE BEACH II

1/3 oz. crème de cassis
1/3 oz. Midori
1/3 oz. pineapple juice

Shake and strain into a shot glass.

———— •—◆—• ————

SEX ON THE BEACH III

1 oz. vodka
1/2 oz. peach schnapps
1 oz. cranberry juice
1 oz. grapefruit juice

Shake and strain.

SEX ON THE BEACH IV

1/2 oz. vodka
1/2 oz. peach schnapps
1/2 oz. melon liqueur
1/2 oz. Southern Comfort
splash orange juice
splash cranberry juice

Shake and strain.

———— • ◆ • ————

SEX ON THE BEACH V

3/4 oz. Chambord
3/4 oz. Midori
2 oz. pineapple juice
splash cranberry juice

Shake or stir. Pour into a shot glass.

SEX ON THE BEACH VI

Equal parts:
  vodka
  Chambord
  peach schnapps
  cranberry juice

Shake and strain.

———— •◆• ————

SEX ON THE BEACH VII

1/2 oz. Chambord
1/2 oz. Midori
1 oz. pineapple juice

Shake and strain.

SEX ON THE BEACH VIII

1/4 oz. Midori
3/4 oz. pineapple juice
3 drops grenadine

Shake and strain. Top with three drops of grenadine.

———— •◆• ————

SEX ON THE BEACH IN WINTER

3/4 oz. vodka
3/4 oz. peach schnapps
1 tsp. cream of coconut
3 oz. cranberry and pineapple juice

Blend with ice until smooth.

SEX ON THE BOARDWALK

1/2 oz. peach schnapps
1/2 oz. orange liqueur
1/2 oz. ginger liqueur
1/4 oz. coconut rum
1/2 oz. amaretto
3 oz. orange juice
dash grenadine

Shake over ice and strain into an ice-filled glass.

—— •◆• ——

SEX ON THE LAKE

1/2 oz. rum
3/4 oz. dark crème de cacao
3/4 oz. crème de banana
1/2 oz. cream

Stir with cubed ice and strain.

SEX ON THE POOL TABLE I

1/2 oz. triple sec
1/2 oz. peach schnapps
1/2 oz. Chambord
1/2 oz. Midori
1/2 oz. grapefruit juice

Serve as a shot.

———— •◆• ————

SEX ON THE POOL TABLE II

1/2 oz. vodka
1/2 oz. Midori
1/2 oz. blueberry schnapps
1/2 oz. orange juice
1/2 oz. pineapple juice

Stir with cubed ice and strain.

SEX ON THE SIDEWALK

3/4 oz. Midori
3/4 oz. Chambord
1/2 oz. cranberry juice

Shake and strain.

—— • ◆ • ——

SEX ON THE SLOPES

3/4 oz. dark rum
3/4 oz. Southern Comfort
3 oz. iced tea
heavy dash of lemon juice

Serve with a lemon wedge garnish.

SEX UNDER THE BOARDWALK

1/2 oz. peach schnapps
1/2 oz. Chambord
1/2 oz. Midori

Serve as a shot.

— • ◆ • —

SEX UNDER THE SUN

1 oz. Bacardi rum
1/2 oz. Myers's rum
1/2 oz. orange juice
1/2 oz. pineapple juice
dash grenadine

Add a lime twist, cherry, and a paper umbrella.

SHAVED BUSH

1/4 oz. Bacardi
1/4 oz. crème de almond
1/4 oz. Kahlúa
1/4 oz. white crème de cacao
1/2 oz. milk

Shake and strain.

SICILIAN KISS I

1 oz. amaretto
1 oz. Irish cream
1 oz. Galliano

Stir with cubed ice and strain.

SICILIAN KISS II

1 1/4 oz. Southern Comfort
3/4 oz. amaretto

Serve over cubed ice.

———— •◆• ————

SILK PANTY

3/5 peach schnapps
2/5 Stolichnaya vodka

Pour chilled Stolichnaya along with chilled peach schnapps straight into a shot glass. So nice, when so close.

Silk Panty

SIT ON MY FACE

Equal parts:
  blackberry brandy
  amaretto
  triple sec
  Rose's lime juice

Build.

—————— •◆• ——————

SKINNY DIPPER

2 oz. Midori
3 oz. cranberry juice

Combine over ice in a tall glass.

SKIP AND GO NAKED I

1 1/4 oz. vodka
1 1/4 oz. sweet & sour mix
cold beer

Build in a Collins glass with cubed ice and fill with beer.

———— • ◆ • ————

SKIP AND GO NAKED II

1 oz. gin
2 oz. sweet & sour mix
dash grenadine
splash draft beer

Shake all but the beer. Strain and top with beer.

SKIP, RUN, AND GO NAKED

short beer
double shot of tequila
dash of bitters

Mix and drink and run.

———— • ◆ • ————

SLIPPERY DICK

Equal parts:
  peppermint schnapps
  amaretto

Layer.

SLIPPERY NIPPLE I

Equal parts:
  peppermint schnapps
  Baileys Irish cream

Layer.

—— • ◆ • ——

SLIPPERY NIPPLE II

2/3 oz. sambuca
1/3 oz. Baileys Irish cream

Layer.

SLOW COMFORTABLE
SCREW I

1 oz. sloe gin
1/2 oz. Southern Comfort

Fill with orange juice. Stir well.

———— • ◆ • ————

SLOW COMFORTABLE
SCREW II

1/2 oz. vodka
1/2 oz. sloe gin
1/2 oz. Southern Comfort
3 oz. orange juice

Serve over cubed ice.

Slow, Comfortable Screw

SLOW, COMFORTABLE SCREW UP AGAINST THE WALL I

1/2 oz. sloe gin
1/2 oz. Southern Comfort
1/2 oz. Galliano

Mix in a collins glass filled with ice. Fill with orange juice. Stir well.

SLOW, COMFORTABLE SCREW UP AGAINST THE WALL II

1/2 oz. vodka
1/2 oz. sloe gin
1/2 oz. Southern Comfort
1/4 oz. Galliano
3 oz. orange juice

Float Galliano.

SLOW, COMFORTABLE SCREW UP AGAINST THE WALL MEXICAN STYLE

1/2 oz. sloe gin
1/2 oz. Southern Comfort
1/2 oz. Galliano
1/2 oz. Sauza tequila

Mix in a Collins glass filled with ice. Fill with orange juice. Stir well.

———— •◆• ————

SLOW FUZZY SCREW

1 oz. vodka
1/4 oz. sloe gin
1/2 oz. peach schnapps
3 oz. orange juice

SLOW MEXICAN SCREW

1 oz. tequila
3/4 oz. sloe gin
3 oz. orange juice

Pour sloe gin over cubed ice. Add tequila and juice.

— • ◆ • —

SLOW SCREW

1 oz. sloe gin
orange juice

Mix in a highball glass filled with ice. Fill with orange juice. Stir ever so slowly.

SLOW SCREW UP AGAINST
THE WALL

1 1/2 oz. vodka
1/4 oz. sloe gin
1/4 oz. Galliano
3 oz. orange juice

Float Galliano on top.

SOB I

1 part vodka
1 part Midori
1 part Chambord
1 part pineapple juice
1 part cranberry juice
splash grenadine

SOB II

Add peach schnapps to SOB I ingredients.

Shan
Little Rock, AR

— • ◆ • —

SOFT DICK

1/2 oz. Dry Sack Sherry
1 1/4 oz. George Dickel bourbon

Serve over rocks and go to sleep.

SOUL KISS

1 oz. American blended whiskey
1 oz. Martini & Rossi dry vermouth
1/2 oz. orange juice
1/2 oz. Dubonnet aperitif
5–7 ice cubes
1/2 slice orange

Combine all ingredients except 2 or 3 ice cubes in a mixing glass and stir well. Place extra ice in a glass and strain into the glass.

SPANISH FLY

1 part tequila
1 part Cuarenta y Tres liqueur (Licor 43)
crushed ice
ground cinnamon
cinnamon stick

Pour tequila and the liqueur over crushed ice in a rocks glass. Sprinkle with cinnamon and garnish with a cinnamon stick.

Raspberry Spanish Fly

SPANISH MILKMAID

1 oz. Harvey's Bristol cream sherry
1 oz. orange juice
1 tsp. brandy
2 tsp. heavy cream
3 oz. crushed ice

Combine all ingredients in a shaker. Strain drink into a glass. Olé!

———— •◆• ————

SPANISH RASPBERRY FLY

1 oz. vodka
1 oz. Chambord
4 oz. Zima malt liquor

Pour vodka and Chambord over ice. Top with Zima.

SPERM BANK I

1/2 oz. tequila
1/2 oz. amaretto
1/2 oz. strawberry brandy

Shake and strain. Add three drops of Tabasco.

———— • ◆ • ————

SPERM BANK II

1 oz. gold tequila
1 drop half-and-half

Build.

Sperm Bank

SPINSTER'S DELIGHT

1/4 fresh cream
1/4 crème de cacao
1/4 vodka
1/4 brandy

Shake well.

———— •◆• ————

STAB IN THE BACK

2–3 ice cubes
1 1/2 oz. orange juice
1/2 oz. brandy
2 oz. Almaden dry white wine, chilled
2 oz. club soda, chilled
1 thin slice orange

Combine all. Garnish with an orange slice. Look out behind you!

STRIP AND GO NAKED

5 oz. crushed ice
2 oz. rose wine
2 oz. sweet & sour mix
2 oz. club soda

Blend until smooth and slushy. Garnish with lime slice. Drink with shades down.

———— •◆• ————

STRONG HOT SEX

Bartenders Hot Sex
splash vodka

Shake with ice. Serve straight up or on the rocks.

SUCK A DICK

1 oz. George Dickel bourbon
4 oz. lemon juice

Shake up. Serve on the rocks or straight up.

SUMMER PASSION

1 1/2 oz. Alize Red Passion
Perrier or sparkling water
squeeze lemon or lime

Add ice cubes to a highball glass, pour in Alize Red Passion, and fill with cold Perrier. Squeeze juice of a quartered lime or a slice of lemon into the glass and stir gently.

T N T

1 1/2 oz. tequila
cracked ice
tonic water
lime wedge

Pour tequila over the ice in a highball glass. Fill with tonic. Stir and garnish with a lime.

TALL BLONDE

1 oz. Aalborg Akvavit
1/2 oz. apricot liqueur
bitter lemon
slice lemon

Pour first two ingredients into a 12 oz. glass filled with ice. Add a bitter lemon to the top and garnish with a lemon slice.

TEED OFF

1 oz. brandy
1/2 oz. peppermint schnapps
2 oz. pineapple juice
2 oz. orange juice

Shake all ingredients well with ice. Strain over rocks in a 10 oz. glass and stir.

———— •◆• ————

TEST TUBE BABY

1/2 oz. amaretto
1/2 oz. tequila

Add 1–2 drops of cream with a short straw. Serve in a shot glass.

TIDY BOWL I

1 oz. blue curacao
1/8 oz. spearmint schnapps
1/8 oz. Baileys Irish cream

Serve in a cordial glass. This will keep you clean.

———— •◆• ————

TIDY BOWL II

3/4 oz. tequila
1/4 oz. triple sec
1/4 oz. blue curacao
1 1/2 oz. sweet & sour mix

Shake and strain.

TIDY BOWL III

1 1/2 oz. ouzo
splash blue curacao

Combine in a shot glass.

———— • ◆ • ————

TIE ME TO THE BEDPOST

1 part Malibu rum
1 part Southern Comfort
1 part Midori
1 part sweet & sour mix
1 part lemon-lime soda

Traci Strachota and Kurt Williamson
Matthew's Pub, Ranch Bowl Entertainment Center
Omaha, NE

TIE ME TO THE BEDPOST BABY

1/4 oz. Midori
1/4 oz. sloe gin
1/4 oz. vodka
1/4 oz. Southern Comfort
1/4 oz. Chambord
1/4 oz. pineapple juice
1/4 oz. cranberry juice

Shake carefully and tie one on!

— • ◆ • —

UP IN MABEL'S ROOM

1 oz. bourbon
1/2 oz. grapefruit juice
1/2 oz. honey

Shake with cracked ice and strain into a chilled cock-tail glass.

UPA U.S.

1/2 oz. bourbon
1/2 oz. applejack
splash grenadine
4 oz. lemon-lime soda

Serve on the rocks in a tall glass.

------ •◆• ------

URINE SAMPLE

Equal parts:
  Mount Gay rum
  amaretto
  Malibu rum
  orange juice
  pineapple juice

Stir and strain.

VELVET HAMMER

3/4 oz. triple sec
3/4 oz. white crème de cacao
1 1/2 oz. heavy cream

Blend with crushed ice. Pour into a wine glass.

— •◆• —

VELVET KISS

1 oz. Gordon's gin
1/2 oz. crème de banana
1/2 oz. pineapple juice
1 oz. heavy cream
dash grenadine
3–4 ice cubes

Combine all ingredients in a shaker and strain into a glass.

VIRGIN'S KISS

1 1/4 oz. dark rum
1/2 oz. Galliano
1/2 oz. apricot brandy
1 oz. lemon mix
2 oz. pineapple juice

Shake well with ice and strain into an old-fashioned glass over ice. Garnish with a cherry and umbrella.

WET DREAM COCKTAIL

1 oz. gin
1/4 oz. apricot brandy
1/4 oz. grenadine
dash lemon juice

Shake with cracked ice and strain into a chilled cocktail glass.

WET DREAM I

1/3 oz. orange juice
1/3 oz. Galliano
1/3 oz. triple sec

Serve in a shot glass and top with club soda. This one will wake you up.

WET DREAM II

1/2 shot Chambord
1/2 shot crème de banana
orange juice
half-and-half

Shake.

Wet Dream

WET SPOT

1 oz. Cuervo tequila
1 oz. Baileys Irish cream

Shake and strain into a shot glass.

———— •◆• ————

WHIP COCKTAIL I

1/2 oz. cognac
1/4 oz. French vermouth
1/4 oz. Italian vermouth
2 dashes curacao
1 dash Pernod

*Shake with cracked ice and strain into a chilled
cocktail glass. Drink, you fool, till it hurts.*

WHIP COCKTAIL II

1/2 oz. brandy
1/2 oz. French vermouth
1/4 oz. curacao
1/2 oz. Pernod

Shake with cracked ice and strain into a chilled cocktail glass. Not again. This hurts!

——— •◆• ———

WIDOW'S DREAM

2 oz. Benedictine
2 tbs. heavy cream

Combine with ice, shake well, and serve.

WIDOW'S KISS

1/2 oz. Benedictine
1/2 oz. yellow Chartreuse
dash Angostura bitters
1 oz. applejack
3–4 ice cubes
fresh strawberry

Combine ingredients, except strawberry, in a shaker. Strain into a glass. Top with the strawberry. Drink with care.

———— •◆• ————

WILD HOT SEX

Bartenders Hot Sex
splash Wild Spirit

Shake with ice. Serve straight up or on the rocks.

WILD SCREW

1/2 shot bourbon
1/2 shot vodka

Fill with orange juice. Shake.

———— •◆• ————

WOO WOO I

3/4 oz. vodka
3/4 oz. peppermint schnapps

Combine in a glass with ice.

WOO WOO II

1 oz. vodka
1/2 oz. peach schnapps
1/2 oz. cranberry juice

Combine ingredients over ice.

———— • ◆ • ————

X.Y.Z.

2 parts dark rum
1 part Cointreau
1 part lemon juice

Shake with ice and strain into a chilled glass.

"69"

1 oz. Cuarenta y Tres liqueur (Licor 43)
5 oz. lemon-lime soda
1 oz. Seagram "7"
5 ice cubes

12 + 57 (43+7+7) equals 69. This is a mouthful.

69'ER

1 oz. Bacardi light rum
1 oz. DeKuyper Peachtree schnapps
1 oz. cola

Serve your way.

Index